D1499564

Little People, BIG DREAMS™
HARRY HOUDINI

Written by
Maria Isabel Sánchez Vegara

Illustrated by
Juliana Vido

Frances Lincoln
Children's Books

Little Ehrich was a Jewish boy from Budapest, Hungary. He was only four when he and his family moved to America. For him, it was the land of opportunities. He was ready to seize them and live a life full of wonders.

But life was hard in Wisconsin, where the family settled.
Soon, his parents could no longer afford Ehrich's studies.

The streets became his school, and the acrobats and magicians performing on every corner became his teachers.

Ehrich started practicing his own feats in the backyard. He was just nine when he jumped on stage as a trapeze artist. He announced himself as the "Prince of the Air" and flew over the heads of the open-mouthed audience.

He landed at a locksmith, picking locks all day long.
Still, his night shifts belonged to his great passion: magic.

After reading a book by his favorite illusionist, Ehrich honored him with a new stage name: Harry Houdini.

Soon Harry realized that he needed more than card tricks to impress his public, so he used all he had learned as a locksmith to become an escape artist. No-one else could get free of handcuffs, chains, and knots as fast as he did!

Along with his brother, he created a fantastic trick where they exchanged places in just three seconds.

Soon after, he met the love of his life, Bess.
A month later, the newlyweds joined a circus.

The circus was a big rolling family, where everybody
teamed up to bring the show alive.

And the Houdinis worked hard to earn their own stellar moment on stage.

Harry stopped by the police headquarters in every city they visited and dared the detectives to bind him with handcuffs, ropes, and cords. In the blink of an eye, his escapes made it to the headlines of the local newspapers.

But it was by baffling London's police officers during his first European tour that he became famous, and drew thousands of people to his shows.

He even performed for the Russian Royal Family
before returning home as the Handcuff King.

Harry captivated the city crowds, jumping handcuffed from dozens of bridges. Thousands of eyes were watching…

...but no-one realized that Harry had untied his handcuffs before he hit the ice-cold water!

There was only one man who knew the secrets of his genius escape tricks: his chief assistant, Jim. The day Harry was tied upside down and sealed into a water tank, the audience held their breath along with him. And so did Jim.

Harry was the President of the Society of American Magicians when his country entered the war. He taught soldiers how to get rid of restraints if they were ever captured.

And he made an elephant vanish
from a theater in their honor!

Still today, not even the elephant knows how the Great Houdini could make him disappear. It remains one of the greatest mysteries about little Ehrich; the boy who believed that limits are just an illusion and that life is really magic.

HARRY HOUDINI

(Born 1874 – Died 1926)

1890

1899

Erik Weisz was born on 24th March 1874 in Budapest, Hungary. The son of a rabbi and one of seven children, he emigrated with his family to the US, where the spelling of his name was changed to Ehrich Weiss. Little Ehrich took on many jobs to help his family survive after his father became unemployed, including time spent as a trapeze artist. Upon moving to New York City, he learned all kinds of card tricks and realized his passion for performing. While working as a locksmith, he discovered his talent for manipulating locks, and began to develop his act as an escape artist. Inspired by the famous illusionist Jean Eugène Robert-Houdin, Ehrich took the stage name Harry Houdini. In 1894, Harry met and married Wilhelmina "Bess" Beatrice Rahner, and together, they joined a circus.

1908

1915

Talk of his incredible stunts began to grow and Harry, nicknamed "The King of Handcuffs," traveled across the world with his act. No-one had seen anything like it before, and audiences were amazed. Harry devised tricks such as escaping from locked police cells, freeing himself from crates submerged in water, and surviving being buried alive. He also took on challenges set for him by members of the public... including an escape from the belly of a beached whale! During the height of his fame, he starred in Hollywood films and became one of the first action movie stars. He was also fascinated with flight and became a keen pilot. Harry never revealed the secrets to his tricks, and to this day, many of them remain a mystery. Thanks to little Ehrich, we know that the impossible *is* possible.

Want to find out more about **Harry Houdini?**

Have a read of this great book:

Harry Houdini (First Names) by Kjartan Poskitt

If you're in Budapest, Hungary, you can visit The House of Houdini.

Brimming with creative inspiration, how-to projects, and useful information to enrich your everyday life, Quarto Knows is a favourite destination for those pursuing their interests and passions. Visit our site and dig deeper with our books into your area of interest: Quarto Creates, Quarto Cooks, Quarto Homes, Quarto Lives, Quarto Drives, Quarto Explores, Quarto Gifts, or Quarto Kids.

Text © 2022 Maria Isabel Sánchez Vegara. Illustrations © 2022 Juliana Vido.

Original concept of the series by Maria Isabel Sánchez Vegara, published by Alba Editorial, SLU.

Little People Big Dreams and Pequeña&Grande are registered trademarks of Alba Editorial, SLU for books, publications and e-books. Produced under licence from Alba Editorial, SLU

First Published in the USA in 2021 by Frances Lincoln Children's Books, an imprint of The Quarto Group.

Quarto Boston North Shore, 100 Cummings Center, Suite 265D, Beverly, MA 01915, USA

Tel: +1 978-282-9590, Fax: +1 978-283-2742 **www.QuartoKnows.com**

A catalogue record for this book is available from the British Library.

ISBN 978-0-7112-5945-4

Set in Futura BT.

Published by Katie Cotton • Designed by Karissa Santos

Edited by Lucy Menzies • Production by Nikki Ingram

Editorial Assistance from Rachel Robinson

Manufactured in Guangdong, China CC122021

1 3 5 7 9 8 6 4 2

Photographic acknowledgements (pages 28-29, from left to right): 1. Harry Houdini (1874-1926) as a young man, about the time he and his wife formed the team of the Houdinis, Harry and Bessie © Bettmann via Getty Images. 2. Postcard of Harry Houdini in handcuffs and leg irons. © Library of Congress/Corbis/VCG via Getty Images 3. Harry Houdini*24.03.1874-31.10.1926: Erich Weisz (Weiss), escape artist, conjurer. Houdini locked in chains, published in 'Berliner Illustrirte Zeitung' 38/1908 © ullstein bild via Getty Images. 4. Studio headshot portrait of Hungarian-born magician and escape artist Harry Houdini (1874-1926) smiling in a jacket and tie. © American Stock Archive via Getty Images

Collect the *Little People*, **BIG DREAMS**™ series:

FRIDA KAHLO	**COCO CHANEL**	**MAYA ANGELOU**	**AMELIA EARHART** 	**AGATHA CHRISTIE**	**MARIE CURIE**	**ROSA PARKS**	**AUDREY HEPBURN**
EMMELINE PANKHURST	**ELLA FITZGERALD**	**ADA LOVELACE** 	**JANE AUSTEN** 	**GEORGIA O'KEEFFE** 	**HARRIET TUBMAN** 	**ANNE FRANK** 	**MOTHER TERESA** 
JOSEPHINE BAKER 	**L. M. MONTGOMERY**	**JANE GOODALL** 	**SIMONE DE BEAUVOIR** 	**MUHAMMAD ALI**	**STEPHEN HAWKING** 	**MARIA MONTESSORI** 	**VIVIENNE WESTWOOD**
MAHATMA GANDHI	**DAVID BOWIE**	**WILMA RUDOLPH**	**DOLLY PARTON**	**BRUCE LEE** 	**RUDOLF NUREYEV**	**ZAHA HADID**	**MARY SHELLEY** 
MARTIN LUTHER KING JR.	**DAVID ATTENBOROUGH**	**ASTRID LINDGREN**	**EVONNE GOOLAGONG** 	**BOB DYLAN** 	**ALAN TURING** 	**BILLIE JEAN KING**	**GRETA THUNBERG**
JESSE OWENS 	**JEAN-MICHEL BASQUIAT** 	**ARETHA FRANKLIN** 	**CORAZON AQUINO** 	**PELÉ** 	**ERNEST SHACKLETON** 	**STEVE JOBS** 	**AYRTON SENNA**
LOUISE BOURGEOIS	**ELTON JOHN** 	**JOHN LENNON** 	**PRINCE**	**CHARLES DARWIN**	**CAPTAIN TOM MOORE**	**HANS CHRISTIAN ANDERSEN**	**STEVIE WONDER**

MEGAN RAPINOE

MARY ANNING

MALALA YOUSAFZAI

ANDY WARHOL

RUPAUL

MICHELLE OBAMA

MINDY KALING

IRIS APFEL

ROSALIND FRANKLIN

RUTH BADER GINSBURG

MARILYN MONROE

KAMALA HARRIS

ALBERT EINSTEIN

CHARLES DICKENS

YOKO ONO

MICHAEL JORDAN

NELSON MANDELA

PABLO PICASSO

AMANDA GORMAN

GLORIA STEINEM

FLORENCE NIGHTINGALE

HARRY HOUDINI

J.R.R. TOLKIEN

ACTIVITY BOOKS

STICKER ACTIVITY BOOK

COLORING BOOK

LITTLE ME, BIG DREAMS JOURNAL

Discover more about the series at www.littlepeoplebigdreams.com